Abiding in CHRIST

Becoming Like Christ through an Abiding Relationship with Him

PAUL CHAPPELL

First published in 2006 by Striving Together Publications, a ministry of Lancaster Baptist Church, Lancaster, CA 93535. Striving Together Publications is committed to providing tried, trusted, and proven books that will further equip local churches to carry out the Great Commission. Your comments and suggestions are valued.

Striving Together Publications
4020 E. Lancaster Blvd.
Lancaster, CA 93535
800.201.7748

Cover design by Andrew Jones and Jeremy Lofgren
Layout by Craig Parker
Edited by Andrew Jones, Kayla Nelson, and Cary Schmidt
Special thanks to our proofreaders.

ISBN 1-59894-012-0

Printed in the United States of America

Table of Contents

Abiding in His Presence

Key Verses

I am the true vine, and my Father is the husbandman. Every branch in me that beareth not fruit he taketh away: and every branch that beareth fruit, he purgeth it, that it may bring forth more fruit. Now ye are clean through the word which I have spoken unto you. Abide in me, and I in you. As the branch cannot bear fruit of itself, except it abide in the vine; no more can ye, except ye abide in me.—JOHN 15:1–4

Overview

John 15 is a personal invitation to believers from Jesus Christ to abide with Him daily. In this lesson, we will see the supremacy of Jesus Christ, the One who makes this invitation. We will also marvel at the invitation to mutual abiding and savor the amazing love we find in an abiding relationship with Jesus Christ.

Lesson Theme

The Saviour of the world invites us into an intimate, personal, abiding relationship with Him where we will experience His wonderful love.

Introduction

_____

_____

_____

I. The _Supremacy_ of His Presence

A. *Jesus Is the* _I Am_

B. *Jesus Is the True* _Vine_

C. *Believers Share the* _Life_ *of the Vine*

II. The _invitation_ to His Presence

A. *Abide in* _Me_
"For by grace are ye saved through faith; and that not of yourselves: it is the gift of God."—EPHESIANS 2:8

  1. _Bible_ STUDY
"In the beginning was the Word, and the Word was with God, and the Word was God."—JOHN 1:1

  2. _Prayer_
"Draw nigh to God and He will draw nigh to you."—JAMES 4:8

  1 PETER 2:1

3. _TRIALS_

"*That the trial of your faith, being much more precious than of gold that perisheth, though it be tried with fire, might be found unto praise and honour and glory at the appearing of Jesus Christ.*"—1 PETER 1:7

"*Casting all your care upon him; for he careth for you.*"—1 PETER 5:7

B. I in _YOU_ - HEB 13:5

III. The _____ of His Presence

"*As the Father hath loved me, so have I loved you: continue ye in my love.*"—JOHN 15:9

A. _ETERNAL_ Love

"*Herein is love, not that we loved God, but that he loved us.*"—1 JOHN 4:10

B. _PERFECT_ ~~EATH~~ Love

C. _UNCHANGING_ ~~PERFECT~~ Love

"*Who shall separate us from the love of Christ?*" —ROMANS 8:35

"*For I am persuaded, that neither death, nor life, nor angels, nor principalities, nor powers, nor things present, nor things to come, nor height, nor depth, nor any other creature, shall be able to separate us from the love of God, which is in Christ Jesus our Lord.*" —ROMANS 8:38–39

Conclusion

_____

_____

_____

Study Questions

1. What does the word "abide" mean?

2. What are the two words that show God's supremacy in verse one?

3. Who do the branches represent? What about the vine?

4. After salvation, what are three ways in which we can abide in Christ?

5. What trial have you been through lately that has brought you closer to the Lord?

6.   Name at least three burdens that you carry that you can give to the Lord.

7.   List at least five people from the Bible who sinned but with whom God forgave and restored fellowship.

8.   Write out some ways that you can begin abiding in Christ today.

Memory Verse

"For I am persuaded, that neither death, nor life, nor angels, nor principalities, nor powers, nor things present, nor things to come, Nor height, nor depth, nor any other creature, shall be able to separate us from the love of God, which is in Christ Jesus our Lord."—ROMANS 8:38–39

Abiding in His Purpose

Key Verses

I am the true vine, and my Father is the husbandman. Every branch in me that beareth not fruit he taketh away: and every branch that beareth fruit, he purgeth it, that it may bring forth more fruit. Now ye are clean through the word which I have spoken unto you. Abide in me, and I in you. As the branch cannot bear fruit of itself, except it abide in the vine; no more can ye except ye, abide in me. I am the vine, ye are the branches: He that abideth in me, and I in him, the same bringeth forth much fruit; for without me ye can do nothing. If a man abide not in me, he is cast forth as a branch, and is withered; and men gather them, and cast them into the fire, and they are burned. If ye abide in me, and my words abide in you, ye shall ask what ye will, and it shall be done unto you. Herein is my Father glorified, that ye bear much fruit; so shall ye be my disciples.—JOHN 15:1–8

Overview

After salvation, God calls the Christian into an abiding relationship with Jesus Christ. This relationship involves living for an eternal purpose. This lesson will help the Christian understand the basic principles of God's purpose for their lives—to bear fruit. Aligning our lives with His purpose will bring forth much fruit for the glory of God.

Lesson Theme

Abiding in a relationship with Jesus Christ will change your purpose for living and will bear fruit for the glory of God.

Introduction

_____

_____

_____

"Hereafter I will not talk much with you: for the prince of this world cometh, and hath nothing in me."—JOHN 14:30

"Even the Spirit of truth; whom the world cannot receive, because it seeth him not, neither knoweth him: but ye know him; for he dwelleth with you, and shall be in you."
—JOHN 14:17

I. The _Purpose_ of the Abiding Christian

A. God's Purpose for My Life Is that I Will
Bear fruit

"Every branch in me that beareth not fruit he taketh away: and every branch that beareth fruit, he purgeth it, that it may bring forth more fruit."
—JOHN 15:2

"Ye have not chosen me, but I have chosen you, and ordained you, that ye should go and bring forth fruit, and that your fruit should remain…."—JOHN 15:16

"And let ours also learn to maintain good works for necessary uses, that they be not unfruitful."
—TITUS 3:14

"Blessed is the man that walketh not in the counsel of the ungodly, nor standeth in the way of sinners,

nor sitteth in the seat of the scornful. But his delight is in the law of the LORD ; and in his law doth he meditate day and night. And he shall be like a tree planted by the rivers of water, that bringeth forth his fruit in his season; his leaf also shall not wither; and whatsoever he doeth shall prosper."—PSALM 1:1–3

B. Abiding in His Person Will Lead Me To _Know_ and _fulfill_ His Purpose

"Those that be planted in the house of the Lord shall flourish in the courts of our God. They shall bring forth fruit in old age; they shall be fat and flourishing."—PSALM 92:13–14

II. The _Product_ of an Abiding Christian

A. The _Fruit_ of the Spirit

"But the fruit of the Spirit is love, joy, peace, longsuffering, gentleness, goodness, faith, Meekness, temperance: against such there is no law."
—GALATIANS 5:22–23

1. _Love - Unconditional, Sacrificial meeting of a need of someone else_
2. _Joy_
3. _Peace_
4. _Longsuffering_
5. _Gentleness_
6. _Goodness_
7. _Faith_
8. _Meekness_
9. _Temperance_

B. Bringing _____ to Christ

"*The fruit of the righteous is a tree of life; and he that winneth souls is wise.*"—PROVERBS 11:30

"*They that sow in tears shall reap in joy. He that goeth forth and weepeth, bearing precious seed, shall doubtless come again with rejoicing, bringing his sheaves with him.*"—PSALM 126:5–6

III. The _____ of the Abiding Christian

"*Herein is my Father glorified, that ye bear much fruit; so shall ye be my disciples.*"—JOHN 15:8

A. _____

B. As a _____

Conclusion

_____

_____

_____

Study Questions

1. According to John 15, what is God's purpose for the Christian?

2. What are the two types of fruit-bearing?

3. Who is the water source for us as Christians?

4. Where should all praise go?

5. Think about the fruit of your own life. How would you describe your relationship to the source of the water supply?

6. What weeds of sin do you need to pull from your life today?

7. List the nine fruits of the spirit and write out next to each, what you can do to show each one in your life today.

8. Write out the names of at least three unsaved people you know with whom you can go visit this week and share the Gospel.

Memory Verse

"But the fruit of the Spirit is love, joy, peace, longsuffering, gentleness, goodness, faith, Meekness, temperance: against such there is no law."—GALATIANS 5:22–23

Abiding in His Purging

Key Verses

I am the true vine, and my Father is the husbandman. Every branch in me that beareth not fruit he taketh away: and every branch that beareth fruit, he purgeth it, that it may bring forth more fruit. Now ye are clean through the word which I have spoken unto you. Abide in me, and I in you. As the branch cannot bear fruit of itself, except it abide in the vine; no more can ye except ye, abide in me. I am the vine, ye are the branches: He that abideth in me, and I in him, the same bringeth forth much fruit; for without me ye can do nothing. If a man abide not in me, he is cast forth as a branch, and is withered; and men gather them, and cast them into the fire, and they are burned.—JOHN 15:1–6

Overview

If you have ever grown fruit trees, you know that before you can enjoy the product, there must be a time of purging. In the same way, the Christian life requires purging. Before you can experience the product of abundant fruit, God must purge your life by His grace. He will do this through His Word, through prayer, and through trials. He promises strength and grace during the purging, and He promises more abundant blessings and fruitfulness after the purging.

Lesson Theme

A fruitful Christian life requires purging, and an abiding relationship in Christ will sustain us during purging times.

Introduction

_____

_____

_____

"And he shall be like a tree planted by the rivers of water, that bringeth forth his fruit in his season; his leaf also shall not wither; and whatsoever he doeth shall prosper."—PSALM 1:3

"But he that received seed into the good ground is he that heareth the word, and understandeth it; which also beareth fruit, and bringeth forth, some an hundredfold, some sixty, some thirty."—MATTHEW 13:23

"Give, and it shall be given unto you; good measure, pressed down, and shaken together, and running over, shall men give into your bosom. For with the same measure that ye mete withal it shall be measured to you again."—LUKE 6:38

I. Purging _____ the Providence of God

A. God Is the _____

"I am the true vine, and my Father is the husbandman."—JOHN 15:1

"For whom the Lord loveth he chasteneth, and scourgeth every son whom he receiveth. If ye endure chastening, God dealeth with you as with sons; for what son is he whom the father chasteneth not? But if ye be without chastisement, whereof all are partakers, then are ye bastards, and not sons."—HEBREWS 12:6–8

B. He Has _____ over the Branches

    1. HE CAN TAKE AN _____ BRANCH AWAY.

    2. HE CAN PRUNE A _____ BRANCH.

II. Purging _____ the Productivity of God's People

A. By _____ the Object of Affection Between You and God

"And not only so, but we glory in tribulations also: knowing that tribulation worketh patience; And patience, experience; and experience, hope: And hope maketh not ashamed; because the love of God is shed abroad in our hearts by the Holy Ghost which is given to us."—ROMANS 5:3–5

B. By Keeping Us _____ to the Vine

III. Purging _____ the Purification of God's People

A. They Had Been Cleansed As a _____

"Now ye are clean through the word which I have spoken unto you."—JOHN 15:3

B. They Had Been Cleansed _____ By the Word

"For the word of God is quick, and powerful, and sharper than any twoedged sword, piercing even to

the dividing asunder of soul and spirit, and of the joints and marrow, and is a discerner of the thoughts and intents of the heart."—HEBREWS 4:12

"That the trial of your faith, being much more precious than of gold that perisheth, though it be tried with fire, might be found unto praise and honour and glory at the appearing of Jesus Christ."
—1 PETER 1:7

"But let patience have her perfect work, that ye may be perfect and entire, wanting nothing."—JAMES 1:4

Conclusion

_____

_____

_____

Study Questions

1. What are two things that our heavenly Husbandman can do to us as branches?

2. Like a dead branch, what will God do to the things in our life that are hindering us from growing?

3. What is the "water" that God uses to help us grow?

4. How does a gardener prune a branch? What are some ways that God "prunes" our life?

5. Explain the unique qualities of the vine and branches that apply so perfectly to us.

6. Write out every problem and trial that you are going through right now. Then, write a thank you note to God for those trials and commit to Him to become a better Christian rather than a bitter Christian because of them.

7. As we see in this lesson, how much you grow is in direct proportion to how well you prepare. How are some ways that you can prepare your heart before the preaching of His Word?

8. List some trials that you went through within the past few years and how your life is better from God's purging.

Memory Verse

"That the trial of your faith, being much more precious than of gold that perisheth, though it be tried with fire, might be found unto praise and honour and glory at the appearing of Jesus Christ."—1 PETER 1:7

Abiding in Prayer

Key Verses

I am the true vine, and my Father is the husbandman. Every branch in me that beareth not fruit he taketh away: and every branch that beareth fruit, he purgeth it, that it may bring forth more fruit. Now ye are clean through the word which I have spoken unto you. Abide in me, and I in you. As the branch cannot bear fruit of itself, except it abide in the vine; no more can ye except ye, abide in me. I am the vine, ye are the branches: He that abideth in me, and I in him, the same bringeth forth much fruit; for without me ye can do nothing. If a man abide not in me, he is cast forth as a branch, and is withered; and men gather them, and cast them into the fire, and they are burned. If ye abide in me, and my words abide in you, ye shall ask what ye will, and it shall be done unto you.—JOHN 15:1–7

Overview

Throughout the Scriptures, Christ indicates His deep desire for us to talk to Him through prayer. He promises to help us in time of need, yet many Christians don't seek His help through prayer on a daily basis. This lesson will help your students understand how God defines prayer, how to pray effectively, and how God responds to the prayer life of an abiding Christian.

Lesson Theme

A Christian abiding in Christ will pray frequently and effectively, and God will respond powerfully.

Introduction

_____

_____

_____

I. The _____ for Prayer

A. _____ *the Lord*

B. _____ *Known Sin*

C. *Exercise* _____
"And all things, whatsoever ye shall ask in prayer believing, ye shall receive."—MATTHEW 21:22

D. _____ *in Jesus' Name*
And whatsoever ye shall ask in my name, that will I do, that the Father may be glorified in the Son."
—JOHN 14:13

E. *Pray* _____

F. *My* _____ *in You*
"So then faith cometh by hearing, and hearing by the word of God."—ROMANS 10:17

"He that turneth away his ear from hearing the law, even his prayer shall be abomination."
—PROVERBS 28:9

"Delight thyself also in the LORD; and he shall give thee the desires of thine heart."—PSALM 37:4

II. The _____ of Prayer

A. Prayer Is _____

"Ask, and it shall be given you; seek, and ye shall find; knock, and it shall be opened unto you; for every one that asketh receiveth; and he that seeketh findeth; and to him that knocketh it shall be opened."
—MATTHEW 7:7

B. Asking Is Subject to _____ in His Will

III. The _____ of Prayer

A. Manifested by God's _____ in Human Affairs

B. Answered Prayer _____ God

"And whatsoever ye shall ask in my name, that will I do, that the Father may be glorified in the Son."
—JOHN 14:13

Conclusion

_____

_____

_____

Study Questions

1. Why do we pray?

2. What are two results of God's Word abiding in us?

3. What are the five prerequisites given for prayer?

4. Why does God answer prayer?

5. List at least three Bible characters that came to God boldly and prayed. Explain what their prayers were and how God answered them.

6.   Make a list of things for which you pray. Study that list and examine your life to see if you are praying for them with a pure heart.

7.   What are some things that stand as a testimony to the power of prayer in your life?

8.   Write out a prayer that shares with God your desire for a better prayer life.

Memory Verse

"The righteous cry, and the LORD heareth, and delivereth them out of all their troubles."—Psalm 34:17

Abiding in His Precepts

Key Verses

I am the true vine, and my Father is the husbandman. Every branch in me that beareth not fruit he taketh away: and every branch that beareth fruit, he purgeth it, that it may bring forth more fruit. Now ye are clean through the word which I have spoken unto you. Abide in me, and I in you. As the branch cannot bear fruit of itself, except it abide in the vine; no more can ye except ye, abide in me. I am the vine, ye are the branches: He that abideth in me, and I in him, the same bringeth forth much fruit; for without me ye can do nothing. If a man abide not in me, he is cast forth as a branch, and is withered; and men gather them, and cast them into the fire, and they are burned. If ye abide in me, and my words abide in you, ye shall ask what ye will, and it shall be done unto you. Herein is my Father glorified, that ye bear much fruit; so shall ye be my disciples. As the Father hath loved me, so have I loved you: continue ye in my love. If ye keep my commandments, ye shall abide in my love; even as I have kept my Father's commandments, and abide in his love.—JOHN 15:1–10

Overview

God's Word should be the foundation and guide in our walk with Christ. Abiding in Him involves understanding and obeying His precepts. As we submit to God's Word, we accomplish three primary goals—we prove our love to God, gain spiritual assurance in our hearts, and promote a loving spirit in the body of Christ. There are great advantages to abiding in Christ's precepts, and this lesson encourages the student to embrace and obey the commands of Christ.

Lesson Theme

An abiding Christian will seek to learn, understand, and obey the commands of Christ found in His Word. Understanding and obeying God's commands establishes a mature spiritual foundation in a Christian's life.

Introduction

_____

_____

"Righteousness exalteth a nation: but sin is a reproach to any people."—PROVERBS 14:34

"This book of the law shall not depart out of thy mouth; but thou shalt meditate therein day and night, that thou mayest observe to do according to all that is written therein: for then thou shalt make thy way prosperous, and then thou shalt have good success."—JOSHUA 1:8

I. Abiding in His Precepts _____ Our Love

"If ye love me, keep my commandments."—JOHN 14:15

"So when they had dined, Jesus saith to Simon Peter, Simon, son of Jonas, lovest thou me more than these? He saith unto him, Yea, Lord; thou knowest that I love thee. He saith unto him, Feed my lambs. He saith to him again the second time, Simon, son of Jonas, lovest thou me? He said unto him, Yea, Lord; thou knowest that I love thee. He said unto him, Feed my sheep. He saith unto him the third time, Simon, son of Jonas, lovest thou me? Peter was grieved because he said unto him the third time, Lovest thou me? And he said unto him, Lord, thou knowest all things; thou knoweth that I love thee. Jesus saith unto him, Feed my sheep."—JOHN 21:15–17

"And why call ye me, Lord, Lord, and do not the things which I say?"—LUKE 6:46

II. Abiding in His Precepts _____ Assurance in Our Hearts

   A. Assurance in His _____

      1. EACH ACT OF OBEDIENCE _____ MY WALK

      2. EACH ACT OF DISOBEDIENCE _____ MY CONSCIENCE

   B. Assurance Builds _____

III. Abiding in His Precepts _____ a Loving Spirit

   A. Love for _____

   "This is my commandment, that ye love one another, as I have loved you."—JOHN 15:12

   "A new commandment I give unto you, That ye love one another; as I have loved you, that ye also love one another."—JOHN 13:34

   B. Love for the _____

Conclusion

_____

_____

_____

Study Questions

1. What can we do to prove our love for Christ?

2. What does obedience to God's commandments bring? What comes if they are rejected?

3. What is the first command of Christ for the Christian?

4. What springs forth from our heart after baptism?

5. Explain the differences between the two kinds of love discussed.

6. According to the first product of abiding in His precepts, how did you show your love for God yesterday? What commandments did you fail to follow, disproving your love?

7. What are some of God's precepts that you struggle with and how can you better obey them?

8. If a love for one another is to come back into our Christian lives, what changes need to take place?

Memory Verse

"Jesus answered and said unto him, If a man love me, he will keep my words: and my Father will love him, and we will come unto him, and make our abode with him."—JOHN 14:23

Abiding in His Pleasure

Key Verse

These things have I spoken unto you, that my joy might remain in you, and that your joy might be full.—JOHN 15:11

Overview

The Christian life is meant to be an abiding relationship with Jesus Christ. The product of that relationship will be full and abundant joy. Christ desires to give us unchanging joy in every area of our lives. No matter the circumstance, our joy can be "full" if it comes from an abiding relationship with Christ.

Lesson Theme

God wants us to experience His complete fullness of joy through an abiding relationship with Jesus Christ.

Introduction

_____

_____

_____

"These things have I spoken unto you, that my joy might remain in you, and that your joy might be full."—JOHN 15:11

I. The _____ for Joy

"Ye shall know the truth, and the truth shall make you free."—JOHN 8:32

A. _____ *the Word of God*

"Rejoice in the Lord alway: and again I say, Rejoice."—PHILIPPIANS 4:4

B. _____ *to the Word of God*

"Although the fig tree shall not blossom, neither shall fruit be in the vines; the labour of the olive shall fail, and the fields shall yield no meat; the flock shall be cut off from the fold, and there shall be no herd in the stalls: Yet I will rejoice in the LORD, I will joy in the God of my salvation."—HABAKKUK 3:17–18

II. The _____ of Joy

"Let this mind be in you, which was also in Christ Jesus."—PHILIPPIANS 2:5

A. His Joy _____ as We Focus on His Word
"A double minded man is unstable in all his ways."
—JAMES 1:8

B. His Joy _____ over Any Heartache
"Looking unto Jesus the author and finisher of
our faith; who for the joy that was set before him
endured the cross, despising the shame, and is set
down at the right hand of the throne of God."
—HEBREWS 12:2

III. The _____ of His Joy
"These things have I spoken unto you, that my joy might
remain in you, and that your joy might be full."
—JOHN 15:11

A. Your Joy Might Be _____

B. Christ's Joy _____ Sin's Thrills

Conclusion

_____

_____

_____

Study Questions

1. What are the two conditions for experiencing joy?

2. How was Christ able to endure the Cross?

3. What hinders joy in the life of a believer?

4. When we are abiding in His pleasure, what does duty become?

5. What did you do yesterday and today that you would have been glad to have Christ return while you were doing it? What activities would you have regretted?

6. According to the world, what circumstances in your life today could cause a lack of joy? What do you need to do to obey God's command in order to have joy in spite of the circumstances?

7. Answer honestly, are you "remaining" and abiding in Him today? What did you specifically read from His Word that kept that relationship fresh today?

8. Write out three verses that speak of the joy of the Lord. Claim these in your life throughout this week, and let them show on your face!

Memory Verse

"These things have I spoken unto you, that my joy might remain in you, and that your joy might be full."—John 15:11

Abiding in His Provision

Key Verses

This is my commandment, That ye love one another, as I have loved you. Greater love hath no man than this, that a man lay down his life for his friends. Ye are my friends, if ye do whatsoever I command you. Henceforth I call you not servants; for the servant knoweth not what his lord doeth: but I have called you friends; for all things that I have heard of my Father I have made known unto you. Ye have not chosen me, but I have chosen you, and ordained you, that ye should go and bring forth fruit, and that your fruit should remain; that whatsoever ye shall ask of the Father in my name, he may give it you. These things I command you, that ye love one another.—JOHN 15:12–17

Overview

God has abundant provision for an abiding Christian. His provision began at the Cross when He provided a pardon for sin. After salvation, He provides a partnership for our lives. He offers us His friendship and allows us to partner with Him in serving an eternal purpose. Finally, He provides a new perspective on life. He gives us an eternal purpose for living and an eternal perspective on every circumstance.

Lesson Theme

As Christians, God wants us to understand and abide in His provisions for our life—a pardon from sin, a partnership with Him, and an eternal perspective on our purpose in life.

Introduction

_____

_____

_____

"This is my commandment, That ye love one another, as I have loved you."—JOHN 15:12

I.   God's Love Provides a PARDON

A.   *All Men Deserve* JUDGMENT

"Greater love hath no man than this, that a man lay down his life for his friends."—JOHN 15:13

"Wherefore, as by one man sin entered into the world, and death by sin; and so death passed upon all men, for that all have sinned."—ROMANS 5:12

"For the wages of sin is death; but the gift of God is eternal life through Jesus Christ our Lord."—ROMANS 6:23

B.   *Christ's* SACRIFICE *Provides a Pardon*

"For if, when we were enemies, we were reconciled to God by the death of his Son, much more, being reconciled, we shall be saved by his life. And not only so, but we also joy in God through our Lord Jesus Christ, by whom we have now received the atonement."—ROMANS 5:10–11

"But he was wounded for our transgressions. He was bruised for our iniquities: the chastisement of our

peace was upon him; and with his stripes we are
healed."—ISAIAH 53:5

II. God's Love Provides _PARTNERSHIP_

A. We Are _FRIENDS_ of the King

B. We Are _SERVANTS_ of the King

III. God's Love Provides a _PERSPECTIVE_ on Service

"Henceforth I call you not servants; for the servant
knoweth not what his lord doeth: but I have called you
friends; for all things that I have heard of my Father
I have made known unto you. Ye have not chosen
me, but I have chosen you, and ordained you, that ye
should go and bring forth fruit, and that your fruit
should remain."—JOHN 15:15–16

A. The Holy Spirit _GUIDES_ Us
"I have yet many things to say unto you, but ye
cannot bear them now. Howbeit when he, the Spirit
of truth, is come, he will guide you into all truth."
—JOHN 16:12–13

B. The Lord Has _CHOSEN_ Us for a Purpose

1. TO BRING FORTH _FRUIT_

2. TO BRING FORTH FRUIT THAT _REMAINS_

Conclusion

_____

_____

_____

Study Questions

1. What is God's divine provision?

2. What are three provisions of God's love?

3. In John 15:14–15, what does "friend" mean?

4. In what specific way do we know we are more than servants, but we are God's friends?

5. Write down the name of someone you love. What can you do for them today to show that love?

6. Explain in a short paragraph the significance of Christ's provision for us, and why we should share that provision with others.

7. Compare some of the ways you spend time with your friends with how you spend time with God.

8. What is some fruit that you have brought forth lately? How can you continue to yield fruit for God?

Memory Verse

"But he was wounded for our transgressions, he was bruised for our iniquities: the chastisement of our peace was upon him; and with his stripes we are healed."—ISAIAH 53:5

God's Perspective on Salvation

Key Verses

And we know that all things work together for good to them that love God, to them who are the called according to his purpose. For whom he did foreknow, he also did predestinate to be conformed to the image of his Son, that he might be the firstborn among many brethren. Moreover whom he did predestinate, them he also called: and whom he called, them he also justified: and whom he justified, them he also glorified.—ROMANS 8:28–30

Overview

God has a master plan for saving us. His plan is eternal, it is in progress in our lives right now, and it will ultimately come to pass by His eternal power. This lesson explores God's purpose in saving us and challenges the Christian to submit to God's purpose and to align his life to God's eternal plan. This lesson focuses on the lifetime process of sanctification through the Holy Spirit and the Word of God.

Lesson Theme

God's plan of salvation leads to the lifelong purpose of conforming the believer to the image of Christ through daily sanctification.

Introduction

_____

_____

_____

I. The _____ of Salvation

*"For whom he did foreknow, he also did predestinate to
be conformed to the image of his Son, that he might be
the firstborn among many brethren."*—ROMANS 8:29

A. To Be _____ to the Image of Christ

1. TO BECOME LIKE CHRIST _____

   *"Beloved, now are we the sons of God, and it doth
   not yet appear what we shall be: but we know
   that, when he shall appear, we shall be like him;
   for we shall see him as he is."*—1 JOHN 3:2

2. TO BECOME LIKE CHRIST _____

B. To Make _____ Preeminent

*"And he is the head of the body, the church: who is the
beginning, the firstborn from the dead; that in all
things he might have the preeminence."*
—COLOSSIANS 1:18

II. The _____ of Salvation

A. He _____ Our Destiny

*"In whom also we have obtained an inheritance,
being predestinated according to the purpose of him*

who worketh all things after the counsel of his own will."—EPHESIANS 1:11

B. He _____ Us to His Destiny
"*Moreover whom he did predestinate, them he also called: and whom he called, them he also justified: and whom he justified, them he also glorified.*"
—ROMANS 8:30

"*Who hath saved us, and called us with an holy calling, not according to our works, but according to his own purpose and grace, which was given us in Christ Jesus before the world began.*"—2 TIMOTHY 1:9

C. He _____ For Our Destiny
"*The Lord is not slack concerning his promise, as some men count slackness; but is longsuffering to us-ward, not willing that any should perish, but that all should come to repentance.*"—2 PETER 3:9

"*Being justified freely by his grace through the redemption that is in Christ Jesus: Whom God hath set forth to be a propitiation through faith in his blood, to declare his righteousness for the remission of sins that are past, through the forbearance of God.*"
—ROMANS 3:24–25

D. He _____ Our Destiny
"*For our light affliction, which is but for a moment, worketh for us a far more exceeding and eternal weight of glory; While we look not at the things which are seen, but at the things which are not seen: for the things which are seen are temporal; but the things which are not seen are eternal.*"—2 CORINTHIANS 4:17–18

III. The _____ of Sanctification

"But ye are not in the flesh, but in the Spirit, if so be that the Spirit of God dwell in you. Now if any man have not the Spirit of Christ, he is none of his. For as many as are led by the Spirit of God, they are the sons of God. For ye have not received the spirit of bondage again to fear; but ye have received the Spirit of adoption, whereby we cry, Abba, Father."—ROMANS 8:9,14–15

A. The Holy Spirit _____ All Christians

B. The Holy Spirit _____ People from the Inside Out

"And be not conformed to this world: but be ye transformed by the renewing of your mind, that ye may prove what is that good, and acceptable, and perfect, will of God."—ROMANS 12:2

"Till we all come in the unity of the faith, and of the knowledge of the Son of God, unto a perfect man, unto the measure of the stature of the fullness of Christ."—EPHESIANS 4:13

C. The Tool of the Holy Spirit Is _____

_____

Conclusion

_____

_____

_____

Study Questions

1. After salvation, we stop focusing on what we received out of accepting Christ and we turn our attention toward what?

2. From God's perspective, what is the purpose of salvation?

3. What does the Holy Spirit use to conform us to Christ's image?

4. What does the fact that He "calls" indicate?

5. Explain how we will be conformed to Christ both spiritually and bodily at His coming.

6. Think about God's omniscience. What things does He already know about your future?

7. How should you, as a Christian, respond to trials and difficult circumstances? Why should your response be different than the world's?

8. Look back over your life and list the steps you have already taken to become more like Christ. What is the next step for you?

Memory Verse

"For if ye live after the flesh, ye shall die: but if ye through the Spirit do mortify the deeds of the body, ye shall live."
—ROMANS 8:13

The Need for Change

Key Verses

What shall we say then? Shall we continue in sin, that grace may abound? God forbid. How shall we, that are dead to sin, live any longer therein? Know ye not, that so many of us as were baptized into Jesus Christ were baptized into his death? Therefore we are buried with him by baptism into death: that like as Christ was raised up from the dead by the glory of the Father, even so we also should walk in newness of life. For if we have been planted together in the likeness of his death, we shall be also in the likeness of his resurrection: Knowing this, that our old man is crucified with him, that the body of sin might be destroyed, that henceforth we should not serve sin.—ROMANS 6:1–6

Overview

Change is never easy or comfortable, and most Christians resist it. We tend to settle into our comfort zones and think "we're doing okay." The first step to becoming like Christ is to admit the need for spiritual change. Every Christian should be on a spiritual growth journey toward maturity in Christ, and this lesson encourages the student to "step up to the plate" and admit the need for Christ-centered change.

Lesson Theme

Lasting change is a need in the life of every Christian and can only be accomplished through humbly admitting that need and yielding to the Holy Spirit's power within.

Introduction

_____

_____

_____

I. We Must _AGREE_ that We Need Change

A. Because of Our _Sinful_ Nature

"This I say then, Walk in the Spirit, and ye shall
not fulfill the lust of the flesh. For the flesh lusteth
against the Spirit, and the Spirit against the flesh:
and these are contrary the one to the other: so that
ye cannot do the things that ye would. But if ye be
led of the Spirit, ye are not under the law. Now the
works of the flesh are manifest, which are these;
Adultery, fornication, uncleanness, lasciviousness,
Idolatry, witchcraft, hatred, variance, emulations,
wrath, strife, seditions, heresies, Envyings, murders,
drunkenness, revellings, and such like: of the which
I tell you before, as I have also told you in time past,
that they which do such things shall not inherit the
kingdom of God."—GALATIANS 5:16–21

"That ye put off concerning the former conversation
the old man, which is corrupt according to the
deceitful lusts; And be renewed in the spirit of your
mind; And that ye put on the new man, which after
God is created in righteousness and true holiness."
—EPHESIANS 4:22–24

B. Because of Our _SELFISH_ **Notions**
"There is a way which seemeth right unto a man, but
the end thereof are the ways of death."
—PROVERBS 14:12

GAL 5:16-21

RECKON : TO SET TO ONE'S ACCOUNT

II. We Must _Reckon_ that the Lord Is Right

"Knowing this, that our old man is crucified with him,
that the body of sin might be destroyed, that henceforth
we should not serve sin. For he that is dead is freed from
sin. Now if we be dead with Christ, we believe that we
shall also live with him: Knowing that Christ being
raised from the dead dieth no more; death hath no
more dominion over him. For in that he died, he died
unto sin once: but in that he liveth, he liveth unto God.
Likewise reckon ye also yourselves to be dead indeed
unto sin, but alive unto God through Jesus Christ our
Lord."—ROMANS 6:6–11

A. Consider God's Word _IS TRUE_ **for Us**

B. Have _FAITH_ **in the Word of God**
"For whatsoever is born of God overcometh the world:
and this is the victory that overcometh the world,
even our faith."—1 JOHN 5:4

III. We Must _YIELD_ to the Spirit of God

A. Being Yielded Is a _CHOICE_
"Neither yield ye your members as instruments of
unrighteousness unto sin: but yield yourselves unto

God, as those that are alive from the dead, and
your members as instruments of righteousness unto
God."—ROMANS 6:13

"What then? shall we sin, because we are not under
the law, but under grace? God forbid. Know ye not,
that to whom ye yield yourselves servants to obey, his
servants ye are to whom ye obey; whether of sin unto
death, or of obedience unto righteousness?"
—ROMANS 6:15–16

B. A Yielded Life Will ___BECOME___ Like Christ

"Be not deceived; God is not mocked: for whatsoever
a man soweth, that shall he also reap. For he that
soweth to his flesh shall of the flesh reap corruption;
but he that soweth to the Spirit shall of the Spirit
reap life everlasting."—GALATIANS 6:7–8

"For if ye live after the flesh, ye shall die: but if ye
through the Spirit do mortify the deeds of the body,
ye shall live."—ROMANS 8:13

Conclusion

_____

_____

_____

Study Questions

1. What is the first step to change?

2. Why must we agree that we need change?

3. What does the word "reckon" mean?

4. How often must we yield to God's Spirit?

5. Make a list of things you know that need change in your life.

6. Explain the fight inside a Christian that takes place between the old and new natures.

7. List some facts that you need to reckon to be true in your life for victory.

8. Make some kind of a reminder right now that will trigger you to admit, reckon, and yield to the Holy Spirit **daily.**

Memory Verse

"What shall we say then? Shall we continue in sin, that grace may abound? God forbid. How shall we, that are dead to sin, live any longer therein?"—ROMANS 6:1–2

The Way of Renewal

Key Verses

Wherefore, my beloved, as ye have always obeyed, not as in my presence only, but now much more in my absence, work out your own salvation with fear and trembling. For it is God which worketh in you both to will and to do of his good pleasure.—PHILIPPIANS 2:12–13

Overview

As the believer yields to the Holy Spirit and becomes more like Christ, his desires will be renewed. He will understand more about what truly pleases God, and God's desires will become his desires! A Christian who is becoming more like Christ will love God's work, seek God's presence, and abide in God's strength. This lesson will encourage the student to choose to live for God's pleasure above all else.

Lesson Theme

As we conform to the image of Jesus Christ, we will have a greater desire to do God's work by His power and for His glory.

Introduction

_____

_____

_____

I. The _____ for Renewal

A. He _____ a "Will" to Know Him
"For it is God which worketh in you both to will and to do of his good pleasure."—PHILIPPIANS 2:13

"For I know that in me (that is, in my flesh,) dwelleth no good thing: for to will is present with me; but how to perform that which is good I find not."—ROMANS 7:18

B. He _____ Us to Know Him
"Blessed are they which do hunger and thirst after righteousness: for they shall be filled."—MATTHEW 5:6

II. _____ for Renewal
"Seek the LORD, and his strength: seek his face evermore." —PSALM 105:4

"But if from thence thou shalt seek the LORD thy God, thou shalt find him, if thou shalt seek him with all thy heart and with all thy soul."—DEUTERONOMY 4:29

A. With _____
"That I may know him, and the power of his resurrection, and the fellowship of his sufferings, being made conformable unto his death."—PHILIPPIANS 3:10

B. With _____

"*And thou shalt love the LORD thy God with all thine heart, and with all thy soul, and with all thy might.*"—DEUTERONOMY 6:5

"*The young lions do lack, and suffer hunger: but they that seek the LORD shall not want any good thing.*"—PSALM 34:10

III. _____ in Renewal

A. *Abide in* _____

"*Abide in me, and I in you. As the branch cannot bear fruit of itself, except it abide in the vine; no more can ye, except ye abide in me.*"—JOHN 15:4

B. *Abide in* _____

"*That which we have seen and heard declare we unto you, that ye also may have fellowship with us: and truly our fellowship is with the Father, and with his Son Jesus Christ. And these things write we unto you, that your joy may be full.*"—1 JOHN 1:3–4

Conclusion

_____

_____

_____

Study Questions

1. What is God's plan for spiritual renewal?

2. Which direction does God work?

3. What are two ways we can abide in God's strength?

4. What are two ways we are to seek the Lord?

5. Discuss the "will" to follow God. From where does it come? How is it strengthened? How is it kept?

6. Did you have a hunger for God in your devotions this morning? How was that hunger fulfilled?

7. Dwell on God's holiness for a few minutes. Write down some other qualities that describe His holiness.

8. What can you do today to renew the joy of an intimate relationship with Christ in your own life?

Memory Verse

"This I say then, Walk in the Spirit, and ye shall not fulfil the lust of the flesh. For the flesh lusteth against the Spirit, and the Spirit against the flesh: and these are contrary the one to the other: so that ye cannot do the things that ye would."
—GALATIANS 5:16–17

Changed by the Glory of God

Key Verses

Now the Lord is that Spirit: and where the Spirit of the Lord is, there is liberty. But we all, with open face beholding as in a glass the glory of the Lord, are changed into the same image from glory to glory, even as by the Spirit of the Lord. Therefore, seeing we have this ministry, as we have received mercy, we faint not; But have renounced the hidden things of dishonesty, not walking in craftiness, nor handling the word of God deceitfully; but, by manifestation of the truth, commending ourselves to every man's conscience in the sight of God.—2 CORINTHIANS 3:17–4:2

Overview

Becoming like Christ requires dynamic, aggressive change. This is a supernatural kind of change that is beyond our power. This kind of internal change is only possible by the power and glory of God. As the believer experiences God's glory personally, this glory will create true inner change that conforms us to the image of Christ. This lesson will help the students understand what it means to allow the glory of God to change their lives.

Lesson Theme

If we are going to become like Christ, we must be willing to experience dynamic change produced only by the powerful glory of God.

Introduction

_____

_____

_____

"Now the Lord is that Spirit: and where the Spirit of the Lord is, there is liberty. But we all, with open face beholding as in a glass the glory of the Lord, are changed into the same image from glory to glory, even as by the Spirit of the Lord."—2 CORINTHIANS 3:17–18

"And the Word was made flesh, and dwelt among us, (and we beheld his glory, the glory as of the only begotten of the Father,) full of grace and truth."—JOHN 1:14

I. Experiencing His Glory Is _____

A. *We Realize that We Fall _____ of His Glory*
"For all have sinned, and come short of the glory of God."—ROMANS 3:23

B. *We Realize that in His _____ He Loved Us*
"When I consider thy heavens, the work of thy fingers, the moon and the stars, which thou hast ordained; What is man, that thou art mindful of him? and the son of man, that thou visitest him?"—PSALM 8:3–4

II. Experiencing His Glory Is _____

A. _____
"Whom having not seen, ye love; in whom, though now ye see him not, yet believing, ye rejoice with joy unspeakable and full of glory."—1 PETER 1:8

B. _____

"And the peace of God, which passeth all understanding, shall keep your hearts and minds through Christ Jesus."—PHILIPPIANS 4:7

"Come unto me, all ye that labour and are heavy laden, and I will give you rest. Take my yoke upon you, and learn of me; for I am meek and lowly in heart: and ye shall find rest unto your souls. For my yoke is easy, and my burden is light."—MATTHEW 11:28–30

III. Experiencing His Glory Is _____

A. *We Are Compelled To* _____ *Him*

1. SERVE HIM _____

2. SERVE HIM _____

B. *We Are Compelled To* _____ *Him*

C. *We Are Compelled To* _____ *Him*

"Let your light so shine before men, that they may see your good works, and glorify your Father which is in heaven."—MATTHEW 5:16

Conclusion

_____

_____

_____

Study Questions

1. What does the word "changed" mean in 2 Corinthians 3:18?

2. When does the growth process stop in a Christian?

3. What is the most humbling experience in a Christian's life?

4. What are three things we are compelled to do?

5. What is the difference between Moses and us in the matter of change and liberty?

6. Find and list three verses or Scripture passages that show God's greatness and man's sinfulness.

7. Make a comparative list of God's greatness with man's lowly position. Meditate on the fact that God loves us and gave Himself for us in spite of ourselves!

8. What should be our true motivation for service?

Memory Verse

"Let your light so shine before men, that they may see your good works, and glorify your Father which is in heaven."
—MATTHEW 5:16

Developing the Mind of Christ

Key Verses

Let this mind be in you, which was also in Christ Jesus: Who, being in the form of God, thought it not robbery to be equal with God: But made himself of no reputation, and took upon him the form of a servant, and was made in the likeness of men: And being found in fashion as a man, he humbled himself, and became obedient unto death, even the death of the cross.—PHILIPPIANS 2:5–8

Overview

Becoming like Christ involves thinking like Christ; to become like Him we must allow our minds to be molded to His mind. The change is first internal, and then expresses itself outwardly. This lesson begins by seeing Christ in His exalted position as God, and then studies His decision to humble Himself to serve and to save us. It concludes by discovering what Jesus was truly passionate about and encouraging the student to have the mind and passion of Christ.

Lesson Theme

Developing the mind of Christ involves humility, serving, and becoming passionate about Jesus' purpose for coming to Earth.

Introduction

_____

_____

_____

"For to be carnally minded is death; but to be spiritually minded is life and peace. Because the carnal mind is enmity against God: for it is not subject to the law of God, neither indeed can be. So then they that are in the flesh cannot please God."—ROMANS 8:6–8

I. His _____

"Who, being in the form of God, thought it not robbery to be equal with God."—PHILIPPIANS 2:6

A. *Eternally* _____ *Son of God*

B. *God in the* _____

"And the Word was made flesh, and dwelt among us, (and we beheld his glory, the glory as of the only begotten of the Father,) full of grace and truth."
—JOHN 1:14

II. His _____

"But made himself of no reputation, and took upon him the form of a servant, and was made in the likeness of men."—PHILIPPIANS 2:7

A. He Made Himself of No _____

B. He Took the Form of a _____

C. He Humbled _____

"Humble yourselves in the sight of the Lord, and he shall lift you up."—James 4:10

"Jesus knowing that the Father had given all things into his hands, and that he was come from God, and went to God; He riseth from supper, and laid aside his garments; and took a towel, and girded himself. After that he poureth water into a bason, and began to wash the disciples' feet, and to wipe them with the towel wherewith he was girded."—John 13:3–5

III. His _____

A. He Became _____

"Saying, Father, if thou be willing, remove this cup from me: nevertheless not my will, but thine, be done."—Luke 22:42

B. He _____ **on the Cross**

"And, having made peace through the blood of his cross, by him to reconcile all things unto himself; by him, I say, whether they be things in earth, or things in heaven."—Colossians 1:20

"But God commendeth his love toward us, in that, while we were yet sinners, Christ died for us. Much *more then, being now justified by his blood, we shall be saved from wrath through him."*—ROMANS 5:8–9

Conclusion

Study Questions

1. What steps need to come before cultivating the mind of Christ?

2. What three things did Christ decide to do in order to come to earth?

3. What is the key word for developing the mind of Christ?

4. What are two characteristics of God's position?

5. What are a few decisions you will have to make today? Contrast the outcome of these decisions when they are made from a carnal perspective and from a spiritual perspective.

6. Describe all that Christ had in Heaven that He gave up to come to earth.

7. What have you done for others today?

8. Why did Christ have to experience the Cross?

Memory Verse

"Humble yourselves in the sight of the Lord, and he shall lift you up."—JAMES 4:10

Living the Life of Christ

Key Verses

I am the true vine, and my Father is the husbandman. Every branch in me that beareth not fruit he taketh away: and every branch that beareth fruit, he purgeth it, that it may bring forth more fruit. Now ye are clean through the word which I have spoken unto you. Abide in me, and I in you. As the branch cannot bear fruit of itself, except it abide in the vine; no more can ye except ye, abide in me. I am the vine, ye are the branches: He that abideth in me, and I in him, the same bringeth forth much fruit; for without me ye can do nothing.—JOHN 15:1–5

Overview

Living the life of Christ is an outward expression of an inward transformation that is taking place by the power of God's Holy Spirit. As we become like Christ, we will not be able to help but show His life outwardly. This lesson examines what the expressed life of Christ will look like in the life of a truly changed Christian.

Lesson Theme

Inward conformity to Christ will always result in outward expression of the life of Christ.

Introduction

_____

_____

_____

I. The Life of Christ Is a _____ To Enjoy

A. *He Is the* _____

"I am the true vine, and my Father is the husbandman. Every branch in me that beareth not fruit he taketh away: and every branch that beareth fruit, he purgeth it, that it may bring forth more fruit."—JOHN 15:1–2

B. *We Are the* _____

"I am crucified with Christ: nevertheless I live; yet not I, but Christ liveth in me: and the life which I now live in the flesh I live by the faith of the Son of God, who loved me, and gave himself for me."
—GALATIANS 2:20

II. The Life of Christ Involves _____ from the Heart

A. *Obedience Is* _____

B. *Obedience Is* _____

"And why call ye me, Lord, Lord, and do not the things which I say?"—LUKE 6:46

"If ye keep my commandments, ye shall abide in my love; even as I have kept my Father's commandments, and abide in his love."—John 15:10

"But be ye doers of the word, and not hearers only, deceiving your own selves."—James 1:22

"If a man love me, he will keep my words: and my Father will love him, and we will come unto him, and make our abode with him."—John 14:23

III. The Life of Christ Is _____ by the Holy Spirit

A. *The Holy Spirit Reveals _____ through the Word*

"But as it is written, Eye hath not seen, nor ear heard, neither have entered into the heart of man, the things which God hath prepared for them that love him. But God hath revealed them unto us by his Spirit: for the Spirit searcheth all things, yea, the deep things of God."—1 Corinthians 2:9–10

"But the Comforter, which is the Holy Ghost, whom the Father will send in my name, he shall teach you all things, and bring all things to your remembrance, whatsoever I have said unto you."—John 14:26

B. *The Holy Spirit _____ Us Away from Sin*

"This I say then, Walk in the Spirit, and ye shall not fulfill the lust of the flesh. For the flesh lusteth against the Spirit, and the Spirit against the flesh: and these are contrary the one to the other: so that ye cannot do

the things that ye would. But if ye be led of the Spirit,
ye are not under the law."—GALATIANS 5:16–18

IV. The Life of Christ Requires _____ by His Grace

A. God Has Grace for Every _____
"And God is able to make all grace abound toward
you; that ye, always having all sufficiency in all
things, may abound to every good work."
—2 CORINTHIANS 9:8

B. God Gives _____ to the Humble
"The sacrifices of God are a broken spirit: a
broken and a contrite heart, O God, thou wilt not
despise."—PSALM 51:17

Conclusion

_____

_____

_____

Study Questions

1. What is the most important aspect of the Christian life?

2. What phrase defines our "relationship" with Christ?

3. How does the Holy Spirit guide us in our spiritual walk?

4. If we are to be good Christians, what are we to obey?

5. Do you have a "relationship" with God today (according to your previous definition)?

6. How do rules apply to a relationship?

7. Take time right now to list some distractions you may have in your life that could hinder your spiritual growth.

8. What are a few things you will just have to endure by God's grace this week?

Memory Verse

"I am crucified with Christ: nevertheless I live; yet not I, but Christ liveth in me: and the life which I now live in the flesh I live by the faith of the Son of God, who loved me, and gave himself for me."—GALATIANS 2:20

Expressing the Life of Christ

Key Verses

This I say therefore, and testify in the Lord, that ye henceforth walk not as other Gentiles walk, in the vanity of their mind, Having the understanding darkened, being alienated from the life of God through the ignorance that is in them, because of the blindness of their heart: Who being past feeling have given themselves over unto lasciviousness, to work all uncleanness with greediness. But ye have not so learned Christ; If so be that ye have heard him, and have been taught by him, as the truth is in Jesus: That ye put off concerning the former conversation the old man, which is corrupt according to the deceitful lusts; And be renewed in the spirit of your mind; And that ye put on the new man, which after God is created in righteousness and true holiness. Wherefore putting away lying, speak every man truth with his neighbor: for we are members one of another. Be ye angry, and sin not: let not the sun go down upon your wrath: Neither give place to the devil.—EPHESIANS 4:17–27

Overview

This lesson builds on lesson thirteen and further examines how the expressed life of Christ will look when lived from the heart. God doesn't only desire inward change, He desires outward transformation that a lost world can see. A mature believer who desires to become like Christ will accept this mission to bring our outward lifestyle into alignment with God's standard in Christ.

Lesson Theme

A believer who is becoming like Christ will be changed both inwardly and outwardly. The life of Christ will be expressed in a renewed lifestyle.

Introduction

_____

_____

_____

I. We Must _____ a Different Walk

"This I say therefore, and testify in the Lord, that ye henceforth walk not as other Gentiles walk, in the vanity of their mind."—EPHESIANS 4:17

A. The World's _____ Condition

1. _____ PHILOSOPHIES

2. _____ UNDERSTANDING

3. _____ OF HEART

B. The World's _____ Nature

"Who being past feeling have given themselves over unto lasciviousness, to work all uncleanness with greediness."—EPHESIANS 4:19

II. We Must Be _____ to Make a Difference

"That ye put off concerning the former conversation the old man, which is corrupt according to the deceitful lusts; And be renewed in the spirit of your mind; And that ye put on the new man, which after God is created in righteousness and true holiness."—EPHESIANS 4:22–24

A. We Must Put Off the _____

"Lie not one to another, seeing that ye have put off the old man with his deeds; And have put on the new man, which is renewed in knowledge after the image of him that created him."—COLOSSIANS 3:9–10

1. THE OLD _____

2. THE OLD _____

3. THE OLD _____

B. We Must Put On the _____

III. We Must _____ Christ if We Will Be Different

"But ye have not so learned Christ; If so be that ye have heard him, and have been taught by him, as the truth is in Jesus."—EPHESIANS 4:20–21

A. Jesus Will Be Our _____

B. Jesus Is the _____

Conclusion

_____

_____

_____

Study Questions

1. In what two ways, given in this lesson, is a Christian to contrast the world?

2. What are three parts of this world's darkened condition?

3. What are some things we are to put off?

4. What are some things we are to put on?

5. List some things to which the world is blinded.

6. What is dangerous physically that was discussed in this chapter? In comparison, what is dangerous spiritually?

7. At what point in your Christian life should you love Christ the most?

8. Today, how are you going to keep from having the sign posted "Business As Usual"?

Memory Verse

"Finally, brethren, whatsoever things are true, whatsoever things are honest, whatsoever things are just, whatsoever things are pure, whatsoever things are lovely, whatsoever things are of good report; if there be any virtue, and if there be any praise, think on these things."—PHILIPPIANS 4:8

Sharing the Message of Christ

Key Verses

Let not your heart be troubled: ye believe in God, believe also in me. In my Father's house are many mansions: if it were not so, I would have told you. I go to prepare a place for you. And if I go and prepare a place for you, I will come again, and receive you unto myself; that where I am, there ye may be also. And whither I go ye know, and the way ye know. Thomas saith unto him, Lord, we know not whither thou goest; and how can we know the way? Jesus saith unto him, I am the way, the truth, and the life: no man cometh unto the Father, but by me. If ye had known me, ye should have known my Father also: and from henceforth ye know him, and have seen him. Philip saith unto him, Lord, shew us the Father, and it sufficeth us. Jesus saith unto him, have I been so long time with you, and yet hast thou not known me, Philip? He that hath seen me hath seen the Father; and how sayest thou then, Shew us the Father? Believest thou not that I am in the Father, and the Father in me? the words that I speak unto you I speak not of myself: but the Father that dwelleth in me, he doeth the works. Believe me that I am in the Father, and the Father in me: or else believe me for the very works' sake. Verily, verily, I say unto you, He that believeth on me, the works that I do shall he do also; and greater works than these shall he do; because I go unto my Father. And whatsoever ye shall ask in my name, that will I do, that the Father may be glorified in the Son. If ye shall ask any thing in my name, I will do it. If ye love me, keep my commandments. And I will pray the Father, and he shall give you another Comforter, that he may abide with you forever; Even the Spirit of truth; whom the world cannot receive, because it seeth him not, neither knoweth him: but ye know him; for he dwelleth with you, and shall be in you. I will not leave you comfortless: I will come to you. Yet a little while, and the world seeth me no more; but ye see me:

because I live, ye shall live also. At that day ye shall know that I am in my Father, and ye in me, and I in you. He that hath my commandments, and keepeth them, he it is that loveth me: and he that loveth me shall be loved of my Father, and I will love him, and will manifest myself to him. Judas saith unto him, not Iscariot, Lord, how is it that thou wilt manifest thyself unto us, and not unto the world? Jesus answered and said unto him, If a man love me, he will keep my words: and my Father will love him, and we will come unto him, and make our abode with him. He that loveth me not keepeth not my sayings: and the word which ye hear is not mine, but the Father's which sent me. These things have I spoken unto you, being yet present with you. But the Comforter, which is the Holy Ghost, whom the Father will send in my name, he shall teach you all things, and bring all things to your remembrance, whatsoever I have said unto you. Peace I leave with you, my peace I give unto you: not as the world giveth, give I unto you. Let not your heart be troubled, neither let it be afraid. Ye have heard how I said unto you, I go away, and come again unto you, If ye loved me, ye would rejoice, because I said, I go unto the Father: for my Father is greater than I. And now I have told you before it come to pass, that, when it is come to pass, ye might believe. Hereafter I will not talk much with you: for the prince of this world cometh, and hath nothing in me.—JOHN 14:1–30

Overview

This final lesson places a powerful capstone on the entire series. This lesson challenges the abiding Christian to accept God's great commission in sharing the message of Christ and equips the student with principles and Scriptures that can be used in witnessing.

Lesson Theme

As we truly become like Christ, we will share His message without reservation to a lost and dying world.

Introduction

_____

_____

_____

"Moreover, brethren, I declare unto you the gospel which I have preached unto you, which also ye have received, and wherein ye stand; By which also ye are saved, if ye keep in memory what I preached unto you, unless ye have believed in vain. For I delivered unto you first of all that which I also received, how that Christ died for our sins according to the scriptures; And that he was buried, and that he rose again the third day according to the scriptures."—1 CORINTHIANS 15:1–4

I. Christ's _____ in Coming to the Earth

"For the Son of man is come to seek and to save that which was lost."—LUKE 19:10

A. Took Him a _____ Way

B. Took Him to a _____ Woman

II. His _____ for Those Who Receive His Gift

"For the wages of sin is death, but the gift of God is eternal life through Jesus Christ our Lord."—ROMANS 6:23

A. To a World of _____

B. To a World in _____

C. To a World in _____

III. His _____ To Provide Salvation

A. His Power Is Seen in His _____

B. His Power Is Seen in His _____

Conclusion

_____

_____

_____

Study Questions

1. What is one of the foundational reasons for becoming like Christ?

2. What is God's promise to those who believe on Him?

3. What was Christ's purpose for coming to earth? Give the Scripture reference.

4. Where are two places that God's power is seen?

5. What are some ways to make people thirsty for Christ through your life?

6. How is the Holy Spirit convicting you about sharing the Gospel with others? How will you respond to His promptings in your heart?

7. What do unbelievers often hide behind to feel spiritual?

8. List some "water pots" that are distracting your witness for Christ.

Memory Verse

"For I am not ashamed of the gospel of Christ: for it is the power of God unto salvation to every one that believeth; to the Jew first, and also to the Greek."—ROMANS 1:16

For additional Christian
growth resources visit
www.strivingtogether.com